T0150965

The
Flood

The Flood

AND OTHER MISADVENTURES OF THE FEMALE PRISONERS OF THE ST. LAWRENCE MARKET

Leah Simone Bowen

PLAYWRIGHTS CANADA PRESS
TORONTO

LIBRARY AND ARCHIVES CANADA CATALOGUING IN PUBLICATION
Bowen, Leah Simone, author
    The flood : and other misadventures of the female prisoners of the St. Lawrence Market / Leah Simone Bowen.

A play.
Issued in print and electronic formats.
ISBN 978-1-77091-937-2 (softcover).--ISBN 978-1-77091-938-9 (PDF).--
ISBN 978-1-77091-939-6 (EPUB).--ISBN 978-1-77091-940-2 (Kindle)

    I. Title.

PS8603.O9735F56 2018   C812'.6   C2018-904729-1
                                                 C2018-904730-5

Playwrights Canada Press acknowledges that we operate on land which, for thousands of years, has been the traditional territories of the Mississaugas of the New Credit, the Huron-Wendat, Anishinaabe, Métis, and Haudenosaunee peoples. Today, this meeting place is home to many Indigenous peoples from across Turtle Island and we are grateful to have the opportunity to work and play here.

We acknowledge the financial support of the Canada Council for the Arts—which last year invested $153 million to bring the arts to Canadians throughout the country—the Ontario Arts Council (OAC), the Ontario Media Development Corporation, and the Government of Canada for our publishing activities.

 Canada Council Conseil des arts
for the Arts du Canada

 **ONTARIO ARTS COUNCIL**
CONSEIL DES ARTS DE L'ONTARIO
an Ontario government agency
un organisme du gouvernement de l'Ontario

 Ontario
Ontario Media Development
Corporation

This play is dedicated to my mother, my grandmothers and those mothers I never had the chance to hold but who made me.

PLAYWRIGHT'S NOTES

This play was inspired by the St. Lawrence Market prison and accounts of incarcerated women in the prisons of yesterday and today. The names and faces have changed throughout history, but the story has not. Women suffering from mental illness, immigrant women, abused women and poor women were those who filled Canada's first prisons. Indigenous and Black people have always been subjected to Canada's criminal justice system at high rates. At the time of writing in 2018, statistics state that Black Canadians are overrepresented by almost 300% and Indigenous people at 500% versus their populations.

The character of Sophia was inspired by Sophia Burthen Pooley. She was an enslaved Black woman owned by Mohawk Chief Thayendanegea (Joseph Brant). Parts of her 1856 life account from *A North-Side View of Slavery. The Refugee: Or the Narratives of Fugitive Slaves in Canada. Related by Themselves, with an Account of the History and Condition of the Colored Population of Upper Canada* by Benjamin Drew were incorporated into the character's monologue for this piece. The character of Mary was created to represent the first wave of stolen Indigenous children who were taken to residential schools beginning in the 1840s. The character of Irish Mary was inspired by accounts of Irish domestics who were often abused and mistreated.

Thank you to Wanda Whitebird for introducing me to the "Strong Woman Song" and speaking about how it originated from the Native sisterhood in the Kingston P4W (Prison for Women).

Most songs used throughout the play are traditional compositions in the public domain, and their scores can be readily found online. The song "Downtrodden Shanty" on page 43 is an original composition, and for information about acquiring music rights and the performance edition of the score, please contact Playwrights Canada Press.

The Flood was first performed at St. Lawrence Hall, Toronto, on March 6, 2016. The play featured the following cast and creative team:

Nicole Joy-Fraser
Brett Donahue
Sascha Cole
Mikaela Davies
Tracey Hoyt
Janet Green
Ryan Field

Directed by Leah Simone Bowen
Design by Rachel Forbes
Stage Managed by Melissa Cameron
Dramaturgy by Yvette Nolan

CHARACTERS

Mary: Mississauga prisoner
Irish Mary: Irish prisoner
Iryna: Ukrainian prisoner
Sophia: Black prisoner
Victoria / Jennie: British prisoner / daughter of Iryna

Guard / Samuel / Fred: prison guard / son of Iryna / husband of Iryna
Various offstage voices

SETTING

Spring 1887
St. Lawrence Market Prison, Toronto, Canada

SCENE ONE

Darkness. Muffled screams and words that we can't quite discern. Water is rushing. The lights come up on SOPHIA, soaking wet. The water gets louder and clearer, as do the screams. She tries to flee but realizes she is chained; she tries to pull the chain out of the wall. We hear the cracking of wood so loud it is almost deafening.

SOPHIA: Robert!

SCENE TWO

Lights up on MARY, kneeling centre stage. She is soaking wet. She spits out a mouthful of water. When she is able to stand and look around her, she realizes where she is and begins the "Strong Woman Song" (traditional).

MARY: Wa-ha / Wa-he-a / he-o!

She pauses, waiting for a response, and then begins to sing again.

Wa-ha / Wa-he-a / he-o
Wa-he-a / he-a / o
Wa-he-a / Wa-he-a
Wa-he-a / he-a-o

> *As lights come up four women reveal themselves, soaking wet. The women are without ailments, pain or any other afflictions during the choral moments.*

Wa-he-a / Wa-he-a / he-a-o
Wa-he-a / he-a-o / Wa-he-a
Wa-he-a / he-a-o
Wa-ha / Wa-he-a / he-o

ALL: Wa-ha / Wa-he-a / he-o
Wa-he-a / he-a / o
Wa-he-a / Wa-he-a
Wa-he-a / he-a-o
Wa-ha / Wa-he-a / he-a-o
Wa-he-a / Wa-he-a / Wa-he-a / he-a-o

ALL: Spring 1887

SOPHIA: A prison

IRISH MARY: Below a market

> *They all look up.*

IRYNA: A women's prison

VICTORIA: Toronto

SOPHIA: Below St. Lawrence Market

IRISH MARY: In Canada

IRYNA: The largest market

VICTORIA: In Canada

ALL: Prisoners

SOPHIA: Sisters

IRISH MARY: Mothers

IRYNA: Daughters

VICTORIA: Women

ALL: Indians

They all look at MARY.

MARY: Mississauga

ALL: We were prisoners

VICTORIA: It was known that the sole responsibility for a woman must be ensured by that of her husband, father or guardian

ALL: Property

SOPHIA: If that woman shall be deemed incompetent

IRISH MARY: Or vexatious in spirit

IRYNA: It is at her guardian's disposal to rehabilitate

ALL: We were property

VICTORIA: Women are persons in matters of pains and penalties, but are not persons in matters of rights and privileges. We must rehabilitate . . .

SOPHIA: Rehabilitate

IRISH MARY: Underneath the city

IRYNA: Discarded

VICTORIA: Below the market

SOPHIA: Between the floorboards

They all look up.

IRISH MARY: We watched the whole of Toronto

IRYNA: Buy and sell

VICTORIA: The animals could smell us

SOPHIA: And we could smell them

ALL: The smell

IRISH MARY: Fresh bread being unwrapped for the stalls

IRYNA: The flower cart making its way to be parked

VICTORIA: The sweet smell of roasted nuts

They all take a breath.

SOPHIA: A cow taking a pee practically over our heads

IRISH MARY: Blood running down the slats fresh from slaughter

IRYNA: The spit and the garbage

VICTORIA: You'd pray for an apple core

SOPHIA: A dropped cigarette

IRISH MARY: A carrot, or a handkerchief

IRYNA: Anything that was different from this place

VICTORIA: This prison

SOPHIA: With chains on the walls

IRISH MARY: For the criminal females of Toronto

IRYNA: Freedom just above our heads

VICTORIA: Hidden from history

ALL: Forgotten

SOPHIA: No records

IRISH MARY: No trace

ALL: We were forgotten

IRYNA: Erased

VICTORIA: Except by one

SOPHIA: Almost

IRYNA: Disappeared

ALL: Except for one

MARY: The voices never stopped

Shift. They all whisper like they are having various conversations and with different intentions.

SCENE THREE

GUARD: Shut up!!!!

The GUARD appears with a very pregnant IRISH MARY. She is wrapped in a blanket. He opens MARY's cell, pushes her in and exits.

IRISH MARY calls out after the GUARD.

IRISH MARY: Thanks so much, sir!

Hello.

She walks up to MARY.

MARY doesn't respond.

I hear they say your name and mine are the same. I'm Mary Kane, well Irish Mary now, and you'll be Injun Mary.

IRISH MARY sticks her hand out to shake; the other MARY takes it.

I knew it! I knew you would be nice! The guard told me that he was pairing me with a Injun 'cause no one else would want me with 'em 'cause I'm bog Irish. But me mum never starved us or gave me away and I can read some letters so I'm not that low.

MARY is silent.

I'm new here.

MARY is silent.

I heard you murdered a priest; is that true?

MARY is silent.

I'm only ask'n 'cause if it's true I could pray for ya. You'll definitely burn in hell, but I'd say a prayer to make sure the fires are so hot that you burn up right away and then you won't feel pain.

MARY is silent.

I'm not here to judge ya though—God knows I've done my share of sinning. I've stolen an apple off a fruit stand like it's nobody's business, and I lied to get over here. My brother Michael got sponsored to come over by Lesmahagow Emigration and I begged him to take me, so we pretended we were married to get on together. That was a sin for sure. I just couldn't a stayed by myself, we had no one left, so we came over together and then he was killed by the fall of a tree. He was a logger. God rest his soul. So you're an Injun? What's that like? Can you really kill a bear with your hands? That's what I've heard your people do.

I'm talking too much, ain't I? I am, I am, it's been a problem since I've been young. Me ma would say I could catch more flies with my mouth than with a gallon of honey. I guess you make me nervous. I can tell you don't mean to but being all silent the way you are it just makes me nervous not to hear your voice, so I'm just filling in the space . . .

Pause.

Did you kill a priest then?

MARY: Why are you here?

IRISH MARY: Oh! Thank you! Thank you for speaking to me! I'm not really here like a criminal. It's 'cause I enticed my employer Mr. Clarke, but God knows I didn't even know that I was enticing until he started coming at me in my room and told me I was. The other maid, Annie, she told me the best thing to do was to pretend I was sleeping, so that's what I would do. It didn't help though. He still came at me left, right and centre. But God knows our sins, and Mr. Clarke said I did sin and now I have my cross to bear.

   IRISH MARY reveals she is pregnant.

I'm pretty far along, I think.

MARY: You're almost there.

IRISH MARY: Am I for sure? How do you know? I've tried to get help but everyone treats me like I have the plague, and I've never had a baby before, nor have I seen it happen. I would run as fast as I could away from any animal that was ready to give birth.

I know it's natural and I have to accept it, but it just seems terrible to me that God didn't make babies just from the sky or somethin' so mothers could just hold out their hands and they would just drop down, instead of the way they come, through you. I don't think it's right.

MARY: I'm afraid there's nothing you can do to change that; babies are born the same way for everybody.

IRISH MARY: Not for hen's though.

MARY: Yes. Hen's have to give birth to an egg.

IRISH MARY: Oh, I guess I never thought about it that way . . .

MARY: Actually hen's have it worse because they lay a bunch of eggs, not just one at a time.

IRISH MARY: I think it's better though because an egg is smooth, and a baby has arms and things that can get in the way on the way out, don't they? When an egg hatches the mother hen just stands there and watches all the poky bits coming through the shell thanking God it's not coming through her.

MARY: I don't think chickens are smart enough to know what they're missing.

IRISH MARY: They're smarter than you think. We had a chicken growing up called Doreen and everyone swore she could say yes or no—that's why she lived so long. The first time me brother went to kill her he lifted the hatchet and she screamed "no"! No! He was so startled he dropped her. Before she ran off she looked straight at him and said "yes"! So he let her go and called her Doreen.

MARY: I have never heard of a talking chicken.

IRISH MARY: Of course you haven't; they are rare, but they do exist. So how will I know when the baby's ready?

MARY: You'll know.

IRISH MARY: I'm was hoping Mr. Clarke would let me out before I have it, but he said I'd need to have it down here. I'm hoping he'll change his mind though. He said he'd come get me after it's born; he just couldn't risk me shaming his wife and position in the community. When are you getting out?

MARY: When I die or this place burns down.

IRISH MARY: Don't say that. Everyone has a path to redemption; I mean that is if you didn't do what they said you did . . . So did ya do it?

Silence.

That guard seemed quite nice. I'll see if I can't ask Mr. Clarke ta help you when he comes for me. I don't think people would mind a redskin working for 'em. I work laundry so ya can help me. We're never seen so nobody could be offended by ya. Would ya do it?

MARY: If your Mr. Clarke ever comes down here, Irish Mary, I would take a walk with him in a second.

SCENE FOUR

*Day. The market is busy. Lights up on IRYNA and
VICTORIA. VICTORIA sits in the corner in some hay.*

OFFSTAGE VOICE ONE: Whole hogs, pigs' feet and bacon!

OFFSTAGE VOICE TWO: A dozen for a dime! Get 'em here a
dozen for a dime!

*VICTORIA starts to choke on her own saliva. IRYNA rushes to
help her.*

VICTORIA: eeeee-ea-eath eathe

IRYNA: Okay, okay. It's okay. Come, let's see what we can
do here.

VICTORIA: eath-eath ah-ha . . . ha!! . . .

*VICTORIA seems to be panicking, trying to make words.
IRYNA bends her forward so the saliva can drain out of her
mouth and VICTORIA begins to breathe normally.*

IRYNA: There now, you're okay; you're all right.

VICTORIA: bre . . . eathe

IRYNA: Yes, breathe, now you breathe. What's your name, huh?
Who's in there?

VICTORIA: et . . . eto-etoia-ia

VICTORIA tries to say her name with little success. She touches IRYNA's face.

IRYNA: Good Lord, your hands are like ice.

Guard, guard! GUARD!

The GUARD emerges from SOPHIA's cell. SOPHIA appears as well, wrapped in a blanket and eating an apple.

GUARD: What?

IRYNA: We're freezing to death with this thaw. This girl needs a blanket or a warm meal.

GUARD: Her days are numbered. We don't waste good supplies on invalids.

IRYNA: Give *me* a blanket then.

GUARD: I don't waste supplies on old wretches either!

The GUARD exits. SOPHIA calls out after him but he ignores her.

SOPHIA: Bye!

SOPHIA watches IRYNA try to warm VICTORIA.

You shouldn't touch her so much—you might as well start digging your grave.

IRYNA: I'm not scared of her; I won't catch anything, that's superstition.

SOPHIA: Sick spreads down here like wildfire, so I know you think you won't get it, but give yourself a couple a days and you'll be flat on your back just like her.

IRYNA: Well that doesn't matter now, does it?

SOPHIA: Suit yourself.

IRYNA: If I don't help it will be thaw that kills her. How do they expect us to live here with this ice water dripping down?

SOPHIA: Who says they want us to live?

SCENE FIVE

Days later. The market is loud, lots of foot traffic, laughter, etc. The GUARD arrives with a pail.

OFFSTAGE VOICE ONE: Potatoes and carrots!

OFFSTAGE VOICE TWO: Apples by the bite and the barrel!

GUARD: Food! Bowls up!

The cell doors open and all of the women step out in line with their food bowls. They are served a grey slop porridge.

Eat!!!

They begin to eat.

OFFSTAGE VOICE ONE: Watch yer feet, boys!!!

A huge amount of slosh begins to fall from above.

SOPHIA: Jesus Christ!!! We're trying to eat down here!!

The OFFSTAGE VOICES laugh, conversations continue from above, more slop comes down.

The women in the prison start to object.

Every day with this. You bloody assholes!! I can see you, you— I know you can see us!!!

More slosh lands straight into IRISH MARY's bowl. She drops it and almost throws up. Fed up she stands on a crate.

IRISH MARY: There are women down here!

We hear the women of the prison agree.

SOPHIA: If I was up there I'd knife all of y'all. Did you hear me? You're dead . . .

*IRISH MARY starts to sing to the tune of "Roll the Old
Chariot" (traditional) to the market above.*

IRISH MARY: Oh we'd be all right if we could eat a meal in peace!

*She encourages the women to join her. We hear many
voices, not just the onstage ones.*

ALL: We'd be all right
If we could eat a meal in peace!
We'd be all right
If we could eat a meal in peace!
And we'll all hang on behind

And we'll roll the old chariot along,
We'll roll the old chariot along

We'll roll the old chariot along
And we'll all hang on behind

IRISH MARY: And no more iron bars
Wouldn't do us any harm!

ALL: And no more iron bars
Wouldn't do us any harm, and no more
Iron bars wouldn't do us any harm,
And we'll all hang on behind

And we'll roll the old chariot along,
We'll roll the old chariot along

We'll roll the old chariot along
And we'll all hang on behind

IRISH MARY: And walkin' overhead won't make us go away!

ALL: Oh walkin' overhead won't make us go away
Oh walkin' overhead won't make us go away
And we'll all hang on behind!

Cheers from the women and silence from above. Everyone goes back to eating.

MARY: That was good; they've never stopped before.

IRISH MARY: They do it on purpose, don't they? It's disgusting, we're still people.

MARY: Here, take mine.

MARY offers her food to IRISH MARY.

IRISH MARY: No, 'sides, it tastes terrible.

MARY: I'm convinced it's old glue, but eat.

IRISH MARY: I can't eat yours.

MARY: You must—we will share then. You need it for the baby.

IRISH MARY: The baby thinks it tastes terrible too.

SOPHIA pulls a cigarette out of her pocket and lights it.

SOPHIA: So, the new girl stops the slosh pouring over our heads.

IRISH MARY: We all did.

SOPHIA: It was fucking brave.

IRISH MARY: I don't think it was bravery exactly, but it didn't seem right what they were doing.

SOPHIA: Oh you're a Shant. I thought they would have another jail for the Irish.

IRISH MARY: What are you sayin'? You're a Nigger!

SOPHIA: A Nigger who was born in these parts, which you ain't, Shant.

IRISH MARY: I didn't grow up in a shanty, and I was working in a nice, respectable house here.

SOPHIA: And you brought shame on the house. When's the whoreson gonna be born?

IRISH MARY: I ain't a whore and I'm not gonna discuss my private business with you, thanks.

SOPHIA: It doesn't look too private to me; it looks like it's arriving soon. Plus, there are no secrets. We're all great friends, aren't we?

MARY: *(to IRISH MARY)* ignore her

> IRISH MARY *begins to eat again but dry heaves.*

Pretend it's fish stew

SOPHIA: *(mocking MARY)* Pretend it's fish stew. Ya certainly smell like fish stew. Imagine, they let a potato-picker live down here with us. I certainly hope you're not diseased.

IRISH MARY: What are you sayin'? You're the one with scabs all over your face—you look like you've got the plague.

SOPHIA: You're a brave little thing, aren't you? Or stupid. I haven't really decided yet. Obviously the wagon-burner didn't explain to you how things work, so let me.

SOPHIA grabs IRISH MARY by the hair.

You don't stand on any fucking crates again to try and pretend you have a place here. Do you understand me, bitch?

This floor you're standing on, food your eating, everything around you is mine. I own it. You're in my part of the cells. I own that invalid, the old hag, the Indian and now you.

They all know if you want to live well and be left alone you don't fucking talk back. Are you listening? Irish whore, tell me you understand?

IRISH MARY nods her head.

SOPHIA shakes her.

Speak.

IRISH MARY: Yes!

MARY: Let her go.

SOPHIA: Oh wonderful, now I have two disobedient bitches on my hands.

MARY: She's pregnant.

SOPHIA: Ring the bells! A cat-lick twat got knocked up, what an event to be cherished.

MARY: I'm just saying leave her be; she don't know better.

SOPHIA: But you do and your still flappin' you ugly mouth—it's all I can do to stand to look at you. Dirty Indian. I know your kind; I know your kind better than you do and I know not to trust you as far as I can spit.

SOPHIA spits in MARY's face to no reaction. She slaps MARY in the face and MARY slaps her back. SOPHIA gets MARY in a headlock.

IRISH MARY: Stop, please stop!

IRISH MARY grabs a piss bucket from the cell and throws in onto SOPHIA.

SOPHIA: You bitch. You harpie bitch!!!!

SOPHIA pulls out a knife.

I'm gonna fucking cut that baby out of you! Do you hear me? I'll fuckin' kill you!!!!!

The GUARD enters and pulls SOPHIA away.

GUARD: Hey!!! What's going on here?

IRISH MARY: I'm sorry, I poured the piss pot over her head.

GUARD: A knife, eh? That means it's the chains for you.

SOPHIA: What are you talkin'?

GUARD: There are no knives allowed down here.

SOPHIA: You gave me this!

GUARD: The rules are for everybody.

SOPHIA: Really!!? That's not what you told me last night, or the night before, or the night before that!!

He punches SOPHIA hard and then grabs her and chains her to the wall.

GUARD: *(to SOPHIA)* You don't know me.

SOPHIA: Please.

GUARD: Everyone back in 'er cell.

He exits.

IRISH MARY: I'm so sorry, Mary; I didn't know. I didn't know she was so crazy!

MARY: It's okay, I should have warned you

IRISH MARY: What's wrong with her?

MARY: I don't know, she's strange. Just don't get in her way. We're on her bad side now, but if we keep silent she'll forget about us soon. Thanks for helping me. I never had anyone stick up for me using a pail of piss before.

IRISH MARY: It was a terrible thing, wasn't it? I'll ask God for forgiveness.

MARY: It was the nicest thing anyone's ever done for me in a long time.

SCENE SIX

Days later. IRYNA tends to VICTORIA.

IRYNA: All right, my dear. It's all right. I'm gonna call you Ermantrude. Do you like that?

VICTORIA: oo-o . . . *[no]*

IRYNA: No? What about Masha?

VICTORIA: oo . . . oo *[no]*

SOPHIA watches from her cell.

SOPHIA: That's not her name.

IRYNA: What is it?

SOPHIA: Victoria.

VICTORIA: e-o-i-a

IRYNA: Victoria, okay, that is what you are saying. How did you know?

SOPHIA: I was upstairs when they brought her in. Her uncle carried her in bawling like a little boy sayin' he was sorry to do it but no one would buy from the family no more on account of them having a cripple and a cursed mute at that. He brought tons of stuff with her.

IRYNA: Like what?

SOPHIA: She came in a wonderful pair of fur-lined boots.

SOPHIA reveals the boots.

And a beautiful quilt.

She reveals that too.

Her mother made it for her apparently.

VICTORIA: he-ee e-ah-ls, he e-ah-ls!

IRYNA: She steals. Yes. She steals.

VICTORIA: aah ee as aing e ive eh aa i uu, I aa aa i . . .

SOPHIA: Shut it, cripple! It's not stealing if you can't even use it. You can hardly hold your head up. Guard told me he was given twenty dollars to keep her in good food. Can you believe that?

IRYNA: Good food! He's given her nothing. I give her half my rations. Where is your pity? What will you say to God when he sees what you've done?

SOPHIA: No one can see us down here. Especially God.

IRYNA: That's always how the bad can do what they do, if you tell yourself that God don't see you can sleep at night.

SOPHIA: I do.

IRYNA: Enjoy hell. So you have blankets and fruit, the middle of winter you stay warm while we freeze, but hell for you in the end.

SOPHIA: That's right, I'll always be warm! If a guard looks you up and down every day, why not use it?

IRYNA: And all the time I was asking myself, what is it she's doing different?

VICTORIA: Whore!!

SOPHIA: Oh you got that out perfect, didn't ya? My whoring has paid off; at least it has down here.

IRYNA: Disgusting.

SOPHIA: My prannie *(grabs her crotch)* has saved my life. It's the only way I eat in here, and it was the only thing I had out there. How else am I supposed to survive? It's my special gift.

IRYNA: I never heard a woman talk such filth!

SOPHIA: Really? You never used your feminine touch on a man when you were young, or did you always look like that? How old are you, anyways?

IRYNA: Fifty-three.

SOPHIA: Good Lord, you might as well be dead! My mistress died at forty and she seemed ancient. I can't imagine living that long; I hope I don't.

IRYNA: Well, I hope you get your wish.

SOPHIA: How come you aren't scared to talk to me like the other women?

IRYNA: Who says I'm not?

SOPHIA: I do—we're talking, aren't we? Nobody else talks to me.

IRYNA: I think that might be because you terrorize them.

SOPHIA: Maybe.

IRYNA: No, not maybe, it is.

VICTORIA: er-erible

IRYNA: Exactly, you're a terrible person.

SOPHIA: But why aren't you scared?

IRYNA: Because the worst has already happened, my dear. I'm in prison, so if you want to kill me go ahead, I'm already dead.

SOPHIA: You might get out.

IRYNA: I've been down here longer than any of you, almost four years. I'm not getting out—I am here for the rest of my life.

SOPHIA: Don't worry, you're so old the end must be near soon.

IRYNA: What a comfort.

    Pause.

SOPHIA: If you need something you can ask me.

VICTORIA: oots

IRYNA: Her boots, yes, give us back the boots.

SOPHIA: Not her, you. If *you* want something you can ask me? I can get anything. I had a piece of beef last month. Did you know that?

IRYNA: That was before. Will he get you stuff now you're in the chains?

SOPHIA: He will. I know men; they're all the same. I've had meat, cheese, fresh bread even. So what is it you want?

IRYNA: I want the things you stole from her and some broth for her to drink; she can't swallow any of the food we're given.

SOPHIA: I said you—only you.

IRYNA: I don't want anything.

SOPHIA: Come on, just name one thing.

IRYNA: A chair, a chair with arms and a good sturdy back.

SOPHIA: That's it?

IRYNA: Yes, I want a comfortable chair to sit in so I don't have to sit on the ground or on a box. I want my back to be supported.

(to VICTORIA) And then, Miss Victoria, we will have something for us to sit on. We will share.

VICTORIA: ah-ah

SOPHIA: You are as crazy as they say you are.

IRYNA: I look crazy?

SOPHIA: No, but that's why you're here, another crazy old woman who has terrorized her family, or poisoned her husband or some such thing. There seem to be many different theories of how you ended up here.

IRYNA: I opened all the windows in December.

SOPHIA: That's all? Why all the scars all over your hands then?

IRYNA looks at her hands as there is a shift and the lights begin to change. The sound of muffled cows and farm animal sounds, the walls open up and the GUARD becomes FRED Derwicki, IRYNA's former husband. He carries a heavy bucket, and slaps her in the face.

FRED: IRYNA!

Your head's in the clouds. I said take this milk before it turns sour right in front of ya.

IRYNA takes the bucket and watches in amazement as he walks off.

IRYNA: Fred? That day . . .

That day was not like others; it was work, but was hot. Not like summer hot, where you find shade or slip off your corset and feel relief. This hot burned my insides. My throat was so dry that there was not enough water to quench my thirst. I didn't sleep for a year. I used to wait till the house slept and go walking in the night in just my nightgown. Sometimes I wanted to be naked, but didn't want the boys to find me dead, stark naked in a snowbank.

I had ten boys and four girls. The first came at sixteen and the last at forty-two, my body never had rest. Two never saw the sun, one died right in front of me, but I can't pretend like that story is only mine. Every one of us lost one or two, that's how it is.

VICTORIA plays JENNIE, IRYNA's youngest daughter. She walks past her in a hurry.

JENNIE: Ma, I'm out to get the water and fetch the eggs.

IRYNA: Jennie! Jenn!

She waits for a response but gets none.

Jenn was my youngest, a good girl who understood farm life.

And farm life is not like the city where you can get by on one meal. You need food or you'll fall over right in the middle of work. That day Jenn and I got out of bed before four and started first breakfast.

JENNIE: Oats, cream, canned apples and ham.

IRYNA: Easy, I've done it for years, but I was so hot that day and standing over a pot of oats bubbling it was like looking into the gates of hell.

JENNIE: I'll break off some ice for you. It will be like angels floating in your mouth.

IRYNA: And it was. So the boys and husband came in at five, ate, left and then we cleaned and started second breakfast.

JENNIE: Eggs, flapjacks, meat, potatoes, beans, scones and coffee.

IRYNA: Timing is everything for second breakfast, 'cause if you end up putting meat on too early . . .

JENNIE: It will be hard as bone, put the scones on late and they will be all dough in the middle.

IRYNA: I was beat by Fred enough times to learn my lesson about that. So, we start second breakfast. I go to make scones but testing the oven to see if it was ready— I just can't . . .

JENNIE: I'll do it, Ma. Why don't you take a breath outdoors?

IRYNA: I do and pack so much snow in my bosom. I felt it freeze my skin but at the same time it felt like . . . like freedom. So I tidy myself up and head back in.

JENNIE: Ma, you have to change your dress, it's soaked to the bone!

IRYNA: I look down and realize she's right. I was soaked . . .

JENNIE: The boys are coming, hurry, Ma!

IRYNA: I changed as fast as I could. I need to be decent before Fred comes, or else, but I can't get everything off in time, so I put my cardigan overtop.

That was a mistake. Did I need a wool sweater buttoned up to my neck? No.

We sat and I could smell every piece of oil and fat that went into the meal. The steam coming off the coffee making me want to wretch, and all I could think is I need to get out of there, then Fred looks at me and says . . .

FRED: You look a bit peaked, Iryna. Why don't you have some tea?

IRYNA: Tea?! He should have just lit me on fire right then, but I can't say no, so I put the kettle on. I sit and dread the sound of that whistle. I could feel the sweat running down into my bum, the heat is coming in waves. Jennie put the cup in front of me.

JENNIE: (whispers) Just pretend.

IRYNA: So I pretended but really I just wanted to throw it in Fred's face. Then he says . . .

FRED: Soup for lunch?

IRYNA: I nod and smile, and he and the boys get up and leave. Soup. Steaming, bubbling, hot brewing soup.

JENNIE: Try to relax, Ma. I'll do the dumplings.

IRYNA: The wool collar of the sweater mixes with the sweat and started to itch my neck and every turn I make to chop or lift or wash it makes me want to faint. The bloomers, corset, petticoat, the dress, the cardigan, the heat, the heat. I just needed a break, a break from the heat, that heat. So, I walked up to the door and opened it, but it wasn't cold enough, so I opened the windows!

JENNIE: Smashed.

IRYNA: Yes, smashed. I smashed every window in that house. I couldn't stop myself; if only I could have stopped myself! I know that the sight of a woman standing in a kitchen with bloodied hands might be cause for alarm, but jail?

I bore him fourteen children and he had me down here faster than lightning.

SCENE SEVEN

Night. Lightning and thunder, the rain begins to pour outside. IRISH MARY and MARY are huddled into one corner.

IRISH MARY: I just love this corner. If you lean just right you can see the baked goods stalls. What I wouldn't do for a biscuit.

MARY: I would kill for some chicken, or beef, or any meat at all. Look at that underwear!

They watch.

IRISH MARY: What's she doing with all that skirt and hardly no underclothes? It never ceases to amaze me how strange rich people are.

MARY: She's not rich. Always look at the bottom of the shoes and that tells the whole story. No holes upper-class, one hole middle-class, no sole piss poor.

IRISH MARY: Speaking of it, can you do the piss bucket today? It's been making me sick just to go near it. It's freezing today, ain't it?

IRISH MARY holds MARY, who is uncomfortable at first but then warms to it.

MARY: You need to try to keep more food down; you should be hungry closer to birth.

IRISH MARY: I'm starving, that's for sure, but just can't eat. It's the smells down here. The piss and shit and ladies altogether.

IRISH MARY dry heaves.

MARY: You need to try and rest. It's not gonna get better until you relax. Girls are always the worst and the first girl is always really bad.

IRISH MARY: I'm having a girl? How do you know?

MARY: Old Indian teaching.

IRISH MARY: Oh.

MARY: No. You are carrying high. When you carry high, you have a girl.

IRISH MARY: But what do the Injuns say? Your kind knows things about those things.

MARY looks at her.

You know what I mean! I mean instinct-like things. Like what the weather is going to be like and animals and such.

MARY: What do we know about animals?

IRISH MARY: Well, I surely don't know, but I've heard that Injuns know about animals and killing and dancing an' things.

MARY: Do you want to know what I've heard about the Irish?

IRISH MARY: Probably not.

MARY: I've heard you're all drunks, and wild with no manners, and you only eats potatoes and grubs even if you had the choice of meat.

IRISH MARY: Eating grubs instead of meat?! Who would choose that? I see what you're doing, showing how fool it is to believe whatever people say, but you'll have to excuse me 'cause I have never met an Injun before.

MARY: Well, I have never met a *nice* Irish person before.

IRISH MARY: When we get out of here I could introduce you to some real nice Irish folk over in Corktown, by the river. Some of the best people, and you wouldn't believe what they could do to a potato. Me mum was a good cook too and my aunt Ida . . .

MARY: I know, I know, your aunt Ida's soda bread would make you wish you'd never stop eating it.

IRISH MARY: Well, it's true. You know, with all the gabbing I do, you've never told me a stitch about your family. Who taught you all about babies?

MARY: It wasn't my family. I grew up in a school with a hospital attached; I used to sneak in and watch people dying and babies being born all the time.

IRISH MARY: Where was your family then?

MARY: I . . . I don't know. I never knew them.

IRISH MARY: Of course you did. Your half your mother and half your da, so you must know something about them.

MARY: I was taken when I was little; I don't remember.

IRISH MARY: Remembering and knowing are two different things. For instance, I never remembered me pa on account that he died real young, but I know deep down inside we have the same feet.

MARY: What?

IRISH MARY: I look at my feet and I just *know* they are my father Carrig Kane's feet. I know it sounds funny, but after me brother passed, I would look at me feet at night and think, at least I still got Pa here to keep me on two legs. That's what he left me, two strong feet to stand on. So where's your family then?

MARY: I don't remember.

IRISH MARY: Stop being silly. Close your eyes and let your insides tell you.

MARY: I don't remember; I can't tell.

IRISH MARY: What do you *know* then?

MARY: Nothing.

IRISH MARY: Try, listen to the rain, let it clear everything out so you can get back to the beginning. Now . . . what do you know?

Shift. A sound: the rain turns into a lake and the far-away rustling of trees and birds. The other women and the cells disappear.

MARY: That's what I know, nothing . . . silence . . . and a sweet smell, the smell of my . . . mother. My mother . . .

My mother would carry me to the lake, humming.

She hums a bit of the "Strong Woman Song."

I can hear her.

We hear her mother humming.

I am little, maybe two or three, sitting beside the water watching my sisters . . . Oh . . . I had sisters!

There, in the lake, splashing around. I'm not supposed to go in, but I do anyway one step at a time on the cool, slippery rocks. The water is so shallow.

I keep going, balancing on each rock, trying to make it over to the group. I take the next step without looking and plunge straight down. The rocks are disappearing and I sink and start to panic.

We hear echoes of panicked voices.

The water is dark green and I can see my sisters' legs in the distance swimming toward me. It's in my nose and throat and the more I scream the deeper I sink.

I can't swim so I just reach out hoping there is a branch or a hand, but instead there's a . . . a turtle swimming toward me. She's so calm; she's right in front of me. Her little legs going side to side in circles, so steady, it's as if she's saying . . .

"Now you do it, now you. Remember the thing you already know how to do."

So I do, I did. I move my arms and legs side to side, back and forth, watching the turtle the whole time and as we rise together to the surface. My mother grabs me just as I see the turtle vanish.

She saved me. My mother picked me out of that water and carried me home singing the whole time.

Wa-ha / Wa-he-a / he-o
Wa-he-a / Wa-he-a / he-a-o

Wa-he-a / he-a-o

Wa-ha / Wa-he-a / he-o

SCENE EIGHT

The lights fade to black, and a candle is lit. We see the face of the GUARD. He laughs and blows out the candle as a result. He lights another candle and suddenly stands in a very circus-like spotlight.

GUARD: Last chance for the fearful to hightail it out of here. All right then, welcome!

As each woman speaks they have a spotlight flash on and then off them. They all have some extra accessory, a feather in the hair or a bit of rouge. They each sing a different key of "welcome" and then harmonize the last one. This is all very circus-like.

IRYNA: Welcome

SOPHIA: Welcome

IRISH MARY: Welcome

MARY: Welcome

ALL: Welcome!

GUARD: Welcome to the Women's Reformatory at the great St. Lawrence Market. As you know, this area is strictly off limits to the law-abiding folk and especially to you ladies. What you are about to see will frighten, entice and provide your curious minds with all the answers of the dank basement society of reject women.

Now I'll warn you these bitches stink, with all their seeping and weeping it can't be helped, they are . . . Oh pardon me for using the word bitches, but there ain't a better word for 'em. Let this be a lesson to ya ladies, mind your men and your health or you'll end up like these 'uns.

And now I bring you those most unfortunate souls, the cursed ladies of the St. Lawrence Market.

Lights up on SOPHIA, who reveals a wooden knife.

SOPHIA: What I wouldn't give to stick this right in your guts!

GUARD: A Negress, a Black slave girl who succumbed to her jungle instincts. She murdered four innocent white Christian souls and didn't stop there. In this prison . . .

SOPHIA: You won't want to get stuck in a cell with me!!

She stabs the air with her fake knife.

GUARD: Back! Back! The most dangerous criminal however is the one who's lost her mind!

Lights up on IRYNA *looking more dishevelled than usual. It takes her a second to realize the light is on her and when she does she begins to thrash around.*

IRYNA: Aaaaagh!

GUARD: Don't fret, folks, she is restrained for your protection. A crazy woman who terrorized her own family. Who knew one so old could be so violent?

IRYNA: If I wasn't in here I'd be cutting up little children in their beds, poisoning my husband or worse!!!!!

GUARD: A shame to be sure, but not as shameful as one who has given her honour and sullied her reputation. Show us your shame!

IRISH MARY: I'll regret it till the day I die!

GUARD: And I'm sure your bastard child will regret it more . . . It is those types of children, conceived in sin and born in shame, that grow up to be diseased and poorly. Not unlike our next girl. A ghost, a living dead creature, she is a diseased cripple, a grotesque!

VICTORIA: ey ut e i ehe aus I ah y-iiin. I aa oin o e ahied. I ah oohm a ii ami-y. ey ohl y ia-he I ehf. eeae ellll, hi ahm i a-ih. *[They put me in here because I am dying. I was going to be married. I am from a rich family. They told my fiancé I left. Please help, his name is David.]*

GUARD: She speaks in tongues!!! Oh Satan is real! Don't come too close or you too could catch this terrible disease, this affliction. And within this prison it is us, the only ones to take pity on a face that only Jesus could love. Pray for her tonight, pray for her and our most downtrodden of all . . . The Savage!!!

The Indian is only kept controlled by these iron bars. How can one be so bloodthirsty? Tell them your crimes!

MARY: I stole a quilt, a lady's hat, a towel, a pitcher, some beef, raisins, biscuits, tea and sugar.

GUARD: Tell them your crimes!

MARY: I scalped and killed a hundred white men and worst of all I killed a man of the cloth.

GUARD: A priest killer! Oh this seductress, a warrioress! A godless red Indian! A song for the good folks, a song!

The women begin to sing "Downtrodden Shanty."

ALL: We are the downtrodden, sad souls
We have sinned and will burn on the coals

The fairer sex is not us
We are downcast to Hades
To pay for our crimes; we commit!
We're just a bunch of ladies
Ladies, ladies, ladies!

GUARD: Ladies and gentlemen, these are the lowest of our society, to be pitied. Take a close look.

That's right, some so beautiful, some so horrific, but all guilty of criminalizing our dear city. Grab your bucket and let us wash them of their sins!

He throws a full bucket of water right at the women.

SCENE NINE

Night. A faint light on IRYNA and VICTORIA. VICTORIA is lying in IRYNA's arms—her breathing is laboured, she is in pain. The prison is asleep.

IRYNA: Shhhhh, this will pass.

VICTORIA tries to speak but can't.

Don't try, don't try, relax, relax.

VICTORIA begins to panic. IRISH MARY comes to the door of the cell and sings "Leave 'er Johnny" (traditional shanty).

IRISH MARY: Oh her stern was foul and
The voyage was long
Leave her, Johnny, leave her

And the winds was bad
And the gales was long
Leave her, Johnny, leave her

Leave her, Johnny, leave her
Oh, leave her, Johnny, leave her

For the voyage is done
And the winds do blow
And it's time for you to leave her

SCENE TEN

Shift. We hear dripping water that grows to waves.

ALL: A great lake

SOPHIA: At the edge of the market

IRISH MARY: Right at the edge

IRYNA: Boats docked

MARY: Fisherman traded

SOPHIA: Slaves were smuggled

ALL: From that lake

IRISH MARY: Water was drawn

IRYNA: To clean the stalls above

MARY: It poured over us

SOPHIA: Cold

IRISH MARY: Filthy

IRYNA: Piercing

MARY: Unrelenting

ALL: That water

SOPHIA: It rose and fell

IRISH MARY: And that spring

IRYNA: As the snow melted

ALL: We were never dry

MARY: That spring

SOPHIA: The lake was higher than it had ever been

IRISH MARY: A market built on a slant

IRYNA: A market that drained into the street

MARY: And into the basement

ALL: We were prisoners

SOPHIA: Hands and feet numb

IRISH MARY: That spring

MARY: The water came for them

ALL: That water came for us!

SCENE ELEVEN

Shift. IRYNA and SOPHIA sit in a cell together. IRYNA sits on a chair with her feet up on a box. SOPHIA sits on a box wrapped in a blanket. The floor is flooded. We can hear IRISH MARY and MARY laughing off in the distance.

SOPHIA: You can't not speak to me forever. It's been two weeks since the cripple's been dead and I thought someone would appreciate I brought her into the only cell with a chair.

Silence.

Her dying had nothing to do with me . . .

Are you deaf!? I just said I ain't have nothing to do with it. I'm being nice, you old bitch!!!!

I guess if I am not to kill with kindness, I'll just kill.

She puts her hands around IRYNA's throat.

I will kill you.

IRYNA: Go on.

SOPHIA: It's gonna be that easy?

IRYNA: When they moved me in here, I knew if the cold didn't get me then it'd be you, so go ahead.

SOPHIA: You're taking all the fun out of it. You never said thank you for the chair.

IRYNA: Thanks.

SOPHIA: You talk in your sleep, did you know that?

IRYNA: I didn't know.

SOPHIA: Really? Who's Samuel? You talk to him almost every night. Tell me.

IRYNA: There's nothing to tell. I don't remember my dreams. Do you?

SOPHIA: I do. I have one that happens over an' over about killing a cat that's quite good.

IRYNA: Sorry I asked.

SOPHIA: Why won't you tell me about Samuel?

IRYNA: I told you, I don't know what you are talking about.

SOPHIA: Tell me.

IRYNA: There's nothing to tell.

SOPHIA: It's a shame, since there's a Samuel that comes here every month trying to see his mother.

IRYNA: What?

SOPHIA: There's a man named Sam that comes to this prison once a month beggin' to see his old ma.

IRYNA: He lives in Kingston; he would never be able to get here once a month.

SOPHIA: So, you do have have a son named Sam. I thought so. You wanna see him?

IRYNA: What do you know about it? How do I know this is true?

SOPHIA: You're getting ahead of yourself. I think I'm gonna need your help first, before I tell you anything about your boy.

IRYNA: What do you want?

SOPHIA: I want revenge.

IRYNA: Revenge?

SOPHIA: I want that Indian and that Irish twat done in. They're the ones who got me chained here.

IRYNA: No. I am not committing any harm, any crimes down here.

SOPHIA: You don't want to see your son?

IRYNA: You hear his name in my sleep and now want to bribe me.

SOPHIA: That's too bad. You should hear the way he prays up there for you. I hear he has quite a scar on his cheek. How did he get that? Did your husband give that to him?

IRYNA: Tell me what you want.

SOPHIA: I know you don't have it in you to do anything really good. I just want them separated, that's all. The Indian never used to talk, never said a word, now Irish moved in all I hear is babbling and giggling over there. I want them punished.

IRYNA: They were punished; they didn't get a meal for days.

SOPHIA: Do you want to see Sam or not?

Pause.

IRYNA: Yes.

SOPHIA: Well then?

SCENE TWELVE

Dripping water. The GUARD arrives with a pail.

GUARD: FOOD!!!! Bowls up!

The cell doors open and all of the women except SOPHIA, who is chained to the wall, step out in line with their food bowls.

EAT!!!

The GUARD walks off a distance and lights a smoke. They all eat in silence until IRYNA suddenly overturns her food.

IRYNA: Shame! Shame on you both!

GUARD: What is it now?

IRYNA: It's those two. Those two godless souls. They are sinners. I saw them with my own eyes, making like they were man and wife. Committing sins with each other.

MARY: She's lying!

GUARD: That's a punishable crime, ladies, turning your back on men to commit lascivious acts with your own gender.

IRISH MARY: We've never done that, and why would you care anyway, you've committed enough lascivious acts with all of the women down here to fill a book!

GUARD: *(to MARY)* Get in your cell.

He grabs IRISH MARY.

You're a mouthy one, aren't you?

MARY: What are you doing!!!!

IRISH MARY: Please, I'm sorry, I'm sorry!

The GUARD begins dragging her away.

MARY: Where are you taking her? Where are you taking her!?

GUARD: She'll have a nice cell of her own now. Away from view.

MARY: She's pregnant; she can't be on her own!

IRISH MARY: I'm with child, sir. Please! Please! MARY!

SCENE THIRTEEN

Night. The jail is silent. MARY stands at the edge of the cell staring at SOPHIA, who is pretending to be reading.

SOPHIA: You can't kill someone by staring at them.

MARY: I am gonna kill you. Next chance I get, I will take those chains and wrap them around your neck.

SOPHIA: It's amazing you never stood up for yourself the entire time you've been here. You never spoke, and then a white girl comes along and it's all you can do not to shit over yourself for her.

MARY: If I don't break your neck, I'll just beat you to death.

SOPHIA: That makes sense. They don't call your kind savage for nothing. Don't I know it. Don't I know. I'm more Indian than you; I know I am. I used to speak Indian really good—forgotten a lot since I've been in Toronto though. You don't even know yourself. You think Mary is your name? You're a fucking idiot, but I don't feel sorry for ya 'cause it's your people who stole me away from my family.

MARY: I didn't do anything to you. You think I'm the reason you're in here? You're here because of what you did.

SOPHIA: What did I do? I'm in here because they think this is where I belong, same with you. We're always gonna be here, okay?

MARY: We're different, you and I . . .

SOPHIA: You don't have to tell me, but I wouldn't be here if it wasn't for you Indians. I was born in New York and I lived a slave with my parents and my older brother, who, by the way, was the smartest boy alive. He learned to read—he fuckin' learned to read—risked his life to do it and learned anyway. He could play a good fiddle too. One day as I was dancing through the currant bushes and Robert was playin' the fiddle, men came up on us and tied handkerchiefs in our mouths and tied our legs and hands and carried us to a ship and put us in the hull and took us up the river where we were sold to Thayendanegea the Indian King Joseph Brant. The first thing he did was give Robert away as a gift to some other Indians from another tribe.

And then I was alone and living in Canada. There was hardly any white people, only wild beasts and Indians and me. I think I was the first coloured girl here. All by myself. I would close my eyes and hear my momma say, "If they split you up, find a way back." But I was seven. Seven years old.

In New York I was owned by people who were cruel and mean but I was with my family and I could adapt, but with Indians there was no adapting. I never knew what was coming and you know who the worst was? His wife. You Indian bitches don't stop when you scream. I got it the worst when Robert and I escaped. He woke me up in the middle of the night and said, "We runnin'." I don't know how he found me but he did.

And we ran and ran but you can't escape when you in someone else's house. White people know the land with maps and trackers, but an Indian knows the land inside and out 'cause it's his.

They caught us of course, and they beat the shit out of both of us—but Robert got it worse.

We were only gone for three days, and when we got far enough he pretended that he was playing the fiddle and hummed that song he would always play. I laughed so hard when I heard it I started crying. And then I cried so hard that I fell asleep in his arms. I ain't really slept good since. I'll never forget him saying over and over . . . we're free.

SCENE FOURTEEN

The water dripping is louder.

Darkness. The middle of the night. SOPHIA stands over IRYNA with a candle.

SOPHIA: Wake up, woman! Iryna, wake up!

IRYNA: What is it you want?

SOPHIA: I kept my side of the bargain.

Out of the shadows steps SAMUEL, IRYNA's son. They speak through the bars.

SAMUEL: Hi, Ma.

IRYNA: Sam! My boy, look at you! Look at you. Well, not a boy anymore, a man. It's so good to see my Sam.

SAMUEL: I'm so happy to see you. I'm so happy to see you, Ma! I tried to get you out. I've been trying. I came to Toronto to see if I could get you out . . .

IRYNA: I know, boy. It's okay, Sam. I'm okay.

SAMUEL: I know you're not crazy, but I just had to be sure.

He exits.

IRYNA: What do you mean? Sam? Sam! Don't leave!!!!

He returns with JENNIE.

Jenn!

JENNIE: Ma!

She bursts into tears.

You look so awful!

IRYNA: Oh, Jennie! What a welcome.

JENNIE: I'm sorry, I didn't know what to expect. There's so much water in here. You're soaking wet!

IRYNA: It's the thaw. I'll dry out soon.

JENNIE: I made you this.

She reveals a scarf.

I see I should have made a blanket.

IRYNA: It's beautiful, thank you. What fine stitches.

SAMUEL: I pray for you every night, Ma. Every night. I pray that you'll be released and if not then you'll have a few moments of comfort from this hell.

JENNIE: We both do.

IRYNA: I feel it. I feel it. How are the others?

SAMUEL: Good, Don and Joe are both married now.

JENNIE: Don has two babies now, Ma. He named the girl after you.

IRYNA: Married, with babies? And what's the boy's name?

SAMUEL: Peter. You should see the both of them. Peter is a huge thing, and little Iryna, well she looks just like her baba. When we get you out of here, you can see for yourself how well everyone's doing.

JENNIE: We're getting you out, Ma.

IRYNA: You don't worry about that; you need to think of yourselves.

SAMUEL: No, you don't understand . . . Pa's getting remarried.

IRYNA: Oh . . . well, I guess it's no good having a wife in jail. He needs someone to help with the house . . .

JENNIE: How can you say that!?

SAMUEL: It's good news. It means you won't be his any longer. I'll be able to get you out once he's remarried. He has to divorce you to marry again and when he does you'll no longer be his property.

JENNIE: You'll belong to yourself soon.

IRYNA: Is that true? I mean with the law? Because I can't take it if it turns out it's not real . . .

SAMUEL: It's real. I hired a lawyer to look into it.

JENNIE: We've both used any money we had to make sure. We got paperwork and everything.

SAMUEL: As soon as he's married—you're free.

Pause.

IRYNA: So, he's leaving me for someone else and they're getting married . . .

JENNIE: Ma! What he did to you was unforgivable. You're not listening . . .

IRYNA: When is the bastard gone?!

SAMUEL: The wedding is in two weeks.

JENNIE: Just two weeks and we'll be together. Sam moved away and I went with him after what Pa did. You can live with us, right here in the city.

IRYNA: I love you both, so much. You never gave up on me.

SAMUEL: We're as stubborn as you are. Just think, in a couple of weeks you'll be free.

IRYNA: I almost can't believe it.

JENNIE: Can we pray, Ma? Can we pray together?

IRYNA: I'd like that.

They all join hands and begin to pray the Lord's Prayer in Ukrainian. As they continue the water becomes louder.

IRYNA, JENNIE & SAMUEL: Ótche nash,
shcho yesý na nebesákh,
nekhái sviatýtsia imyá Tvoyé,
nekhái pryidé tsárstvo Tvoyé,
nekhái budé vólia Tvoyá
yak na nébi,
tak i na zemlí.
Khlib nash nasúshchnyi dai nam siohódni . . .

SCENE FIFTEEN

Shift. Days later. The water is high and rushing in. From the market above we hear yells and major movement. IRISH MARY is alone in her cell on a crate. She is in labour.

IRISH MARY: . . . Thy kingdom come, Thy will be done in earth, as it is in heaven.

She hears the water flooding and pulls her legs up. She begins to panic.

Give us this day our daily bread. And forgive us our trespasses as we forgive those who trespass against us . . . Mary!!!!!

MARY!!

Off stage we hear the distant voice of MARY.

MARY: I'm here, girl!

IRISH MARY: Mary! I think the baby's coming, and there's so much water in here. I can't stand up. MARY!!!! I don't know what to do.

MARY: Just listen, I need you to listen to me.

IRISH MARY: I'm listening.

Shift. Lights up on MARY, SOPHIA, and IRYNA in their cells. We no longer see IRISH MARY.

MARY: Guard!!! Guard!!! Where is he? We'll all be up to our necks in this soon.

IRYNA: *(to SOPHIA)* Call for someone.

SOPHIA: You've heard me calling for the last hour. They've left us to die here, haven't you figured that out?

IRYNA: What about that girl? She's in labour. Surely they'll come for her?

SOPHIA: Why should they?

IRISH MARY: *(off stage)* AHHHHRGGGG!

MARY: Mary, listen to me, you need to reach down and tell me what you feel.

IRISH MARY: I can't, it's burning, I'm burning!

IRYNA: Mary, can you hear my voice?

IRISH MARY: *(between sobs)* Mary—

IRYNA: I just wanted to see my family. I'm so sorry, I didn't know they'd put you in by yourself.

IRISH MARY: Ahhh! It's burning!!

IRYNA: It's not burning, it's the baby's head coming through. I know you're scared, but listen, I have done this fourteen times and lived to tell the tale, and so will you. Do you understand?

Silence.

MARY: Mary?

Silence.

IRYNA & MARY: MARY?

IRISH MARY: Yes?

MARY: You must listen to us.

IRISH MARY: My heart's gonna jump out of my chest.

IRYNA: It won't, it's just beating hard to let you know you're alive.

The water increases. They move to stand on their chairs and boxes.

IRISH MARY: Arragh!!!!!!!!

MARY: What do we do? She's never even seen labour before.

IRYNA: Push, Mary! Push!

IRISH MARY: I can't!

IRYNA & MARY: PUSH!

IRISH MARY: Arragh!!!!!!!!

IRYNA: That's good, keep that up and the baby will be here before you know it. Can you reach down and feel the head?

IRISH MARY's pain increases. We hear her in pain and moaning and then we hear nothing.

IRYNA & MARY: MARY!

Silence.

MARY?!

Silence.

IRISH MARY: I can't anymore—

MARY: You can . . . Mary?

Silence.

Mary?

Wa-o / Wa-he-a / he-a
Wa-o / Wa-he-a / he-a
Wa-o / Wa-he-a / he-a
Wa-he-a / he-a / he-o

Wa-he-a / Wa-he-a
Wa-he-a / he-a / he-o / Wa

The lights slowly fade on them as we hear muffled screams and words that we can't quite discern. We hear water rushing. The water and screams become clearer and louder as we hear the cracking of wood so loud it is almost deafening.

SCENE SIXTEEN

ALL: Spring 1887

SOPHIA: A flood

IRISH MARY: Below a market

They all look up.

IRYNA: A women's prison

ALL: Below St. Lawrence Market

VICTORIA: In Canada

SOPHIA: The largest market

ALL: In Canada

IRISH MARY: A prison

IRYNA: Full of water

VICTORIA: Full of women

ALL: We were prisoners

SOPHIA: Sisters

IRISH MARY: Mothers

IRYNA: Daughters

VICTORIA: Women

ALL: Indians

They all look at MARY.

MARY: Mississauga

ALL: We were lost

As they say the next few lines they begin to form around MARY.

VICTORIA: No records

ALL: Lost

IRYNA: No headlines

ALL: Prisoners

SOPHIA: All those women

IRISH MARY: Voiceless

IRYNA: Out of their minds with fear

VICTORIA: With pain

SOPHIA: Chained to the walls

IRISH MARY: No survivors

ALL: Except for one

MARY: Except for me.

When the water came rushing through those doors and down through the steps I took a deep breath and let the water take hold. I closed my eyes and prepared myself to finally see my parents again. But instead I felt myself being pushed, floating and then sinking, trying to hold on to a piece of wood or anything at all. I got pushed up into an air pocket and when I finally opened my eyes I realized I was still alive. I could see the sop pails and little bits of paper and fabric that had been keepsakes for so many women float past me.

So I started swimming. I started swimming to find Mary. The water was so dark and there were so many things floating in there, but I eventually found her. One arm wrapped around a rafter, blue in the face. I thought I could save her, but she was gone, and seeing her there like that for some reason made me not want to live either.

She had been my only friend. My only real friend in years, and just then, seeing that beautiful soul so lifeless, made me want to be wherever she was. So I sank down and prepared to let myself drown. And as I almost touched the ground I saw these little legs going side to side in circles, so steady, almost glowing in that water. Her baby was alive, and swimming. Eyes shut, reaching out for someone, so I grabbed her. I grabbed that little girl and we rose to the surface just as the final wave came and pushed us out into the lake. We were free.

I was the only one who lived and they didn't even notice me missing from the dead. We didn't count enough to be written down. So I made off with that baby and we made a life for ourselves. I named her Ida after her aunt 'cause I thought Mary would like that. But truthfully, I always called her Mary. The Mary who swam and saved me.

She grew up well, she did, strong and chatty. She was just like her mum. She was the strongest woman I would know, stronger than her mother and me combined. And with confidence . . . I never knew a girl could have confidence like that.

She stayed with me till the end as I laid there in my eighties. "Mother," she said to me, "it's time to see your parents and Mary Kane again. Two mothers, what a lucky girl I was."

And she held my hand as I walked out to the other side.

So kind-hearted and always smiling, except for those nights when her eyes would fill with tears and I held her as we talked about the mother she never knew. She was so sad she never met her and couldn't remember her. And I would tell her . . .

remembering and knowing are two different things. Just look at your feet, my girl, and know that's what your mother left you, two strong feet to stand on.

   End.

ACKNOWLEDGEMENTS

This piece would have not been possible without the support of Obsidian Theatre, Nightwood Theatre, Native Earth Performing Arts, Toronto's First Post Office, the Toronto Arts Council and the Ontario Arts Council. Thank you to Yvette Nolan for helping me usher these women into being and all the actors who participated in *The Flood*'s development with special acknowledgement to Nicole Joy-Fraser.

Leah Simone Bowen is a Toronto-based writer, producer, and Dora Mavor Moore Award–nominated director. She is the creator and co-host, along with Falen Johnson, of the CBC podcast *The Secret Life of Canada* about the untold and under-told history of the country. Select writing credits include *The Hallway, Nowheresville, The Postman* and *Treemonisha*. She has been a playwright-in-residence at a number of theatres, including Obsidian Theatre, Volcano Theatre, and the Stratford Festival. She is a graduate of the University of Alberta's theatre program.

First edition: October 2018
Printed and bound in Canada by Rapido Books, Montreal

Jacket art and design by Ashley Wong, www.ashlwong.com
Author photograph by Adam Rankin Photography

**PLAYWRIGHTS
CANADA PRESS**

202-269 Richmond St. W.
Toronto, ON
M5V 1X1

416.703.0013
info@playwrightscanada.com
www.playwrightscanada.com
@playcanpress